Bearded Dragon Care

The Complete Guide to Caring for and Keeping Bearded Dragons as Pets

Tabitha Jones

Copyright © 2019 Tabitha Jones

All rights reserved.

Although the author and publisher have made every effort to ensure that the information presented in this book was correct at the present time, the author and publisher do not assume and hereby disclaim any liability to any party for any loss, damage, or disruption caused by errors or omissions, whether such errors or omissions result from negligence, accident, or any other cause.

ISBN: 9781798941041

CONTENTS

Introduction 8

Description..9

    Valid Species..9

    Size 10

    Natural Habitat....................................10

    Lifespan 11

    Differences between the Sexes 11

    Probing 12

    Diet 13

    Availability 13

Bearded Dragons as Pets 14

    Before Purchase 14

    Choosing a Bearded Dragon 14

    Transporting your Lizard 15

    Handling 16

    Toenail Trimming..................................16

Body Language 17

Hygiene 18

Recording 18

Can Multiple Beardies be housed together? 19

Potential Dangers 19

Best Practice when Housing Multiple Beardies .. 20

Housing 21

Vivarium Specification 21

'Furniture' 22

Cleaning 22

Substrates 24

Newspaper and Paper Towels 24

Artificial Grass 24

Wood Chippings 25

Oatbran and Wheatbran 26

Substrates to Avoid 26

Heating and Lighting 27

Primary Heating Source......................................27

Secondary Heating Source 28

Lighting..28

Brumation...29

Feeding and Watering Your Pet...........................30

What do Bearded Dragons Eat? 30

How much do Bearded Dragons Eat?.................30

Pros and Cons of Crickets 31

Pros and Cons of Mealworms...........................32

Gut Loading 33

Dusting the Prey 33

Pinkies and Waxworms 34

Plant Based Food..34

Treats...35

Not Eating? 35

Watering...36

Shedding 37

How to tell if your Bearded Dragon is about to Shed 37

A Moist Shelter 37

Breeding 39

Before the Breeding Process 39

Preparing the Breeding Habitat 40

Preparing the Lay Box 40

The Breeding Process 40

The Laying Process 41

Incubation 42

Hatching 43

Final Thoughts 45

ABOUT THE AUTHOR 46

INTRODUCTION

Before purchasing any pet it is important to understand that as a pet owner you are responsible for the care and wellbeing of your pet. It is important to try and learn as much as you can about the animal you are considering to keep as a pet to make sure that your lifestyle, household and financial status are suited to provide your pet with the best possible care. This guide has been designed to provide you with both precise and concise information about a bearded dragon's basic needs to help you provide your pet with the best quality care practices.

DESCRIPTION

The name 'bearded dragon' refers to a genus of reptiles which contains eight lizard species. The scientific name for this genus is *'Pogona'* and they are also colloquially referred to as 'beardies.' The lizards within the genus gained the name 'bearded dragon' due to the extraordinary 'beard' located on the underside of the lizard's throat. In the wild bearded dragons can commonly be found basking on rocks or on the branches of trees due to the species adept ability to climb. They are found throughout Australia in a wide range of habitats ranging from deserts to shrubland and woodlands. Due to their hardy nature and interesting appearance bearded dragons have become a very popular pet and are fairly easy to care for in comparison to other exotic lizard species.

Valid Species

The following listed eight species are the only lizard species recognized as being bearded dragons. It is important to make sure that the lizard you purchase is a part of one of the following species. If the breeder or pet store is unable to confirm the exact Pogona species it is best practice to not purchase a lizard from that location.

- Pogona barbata

- Pogona henrylawsoni
- Pogona microlepidota
- Pogona minima
- Pogona minor
- Pogona mitchelli
- Pogona nullarbor
- Pogona vitticeps

It is important to note that despite there being differences between the species they are all cared for in the same manner.

Size

Bearded dragons are among some of the biggest lizard species that are common household pets. A fully grown male can grow up to 24 inches (60cm) in length. Females are slightly smaller than males and normally are around 20 inches (51cm) long. Hatchlings are normally about 4 inches in length but it is best practice to not purchase a lizard until it has reached at least 6 inches in length.

Natural Habitat

Bearded dragons originate from Australia in a wide variety of habitats. They are known to live in both arid habitats (such as deserts, subtropical woodlands and savannas) and humid habitats by the shore (such as scrublands and shrublands). As previously mentioned wild bearded dragons are normally found on tree branches or basking on rocks. They are also known to burrow underground to avoid overheating in the hot climate.

Lifespan

In captivity bearded dragons normally live between 10-15 years. However it is not uncommon for a bearded dragon to live up to, and even exceed, 20 years.

Differences between the Sexes

It is possible to assume a bearded dragon's sex based upon its behavior and size (males are generally larger and are more likely to display aggressive behavior). However these assumptions are based upon nothing more than anecdotal evidence that does not take into account the species propensity for having individual natures.

However there is a more accurate methods of determining your lizards sex which is by examining the lizard's hemipenal bulges. The differences between male and female hemipenal bulges are not visibly apparent until the lizard has grown to around 6 or 7 inches in length. A male bearded dragon will have two hemipenal bulges on either side of its tail following the vent. On the other hand a female bearded dragon will have a singular hemipenal bulge in the center of its tail. While determining sex by hemipenal bulges is not 100% accurate it is the easiest and safest way to determine your lizards sex. There is a more accurate, but potentially risky, method which will be discussed below.

Probing

Probing is the only way of 100% determining a bearded dragons sex but should NEVER be performed by anyone other than a trained vet who has a long history in the MEDICAL care of lizards. Probing is the process of forcing open the lizards vent and pulling the lizard's sex organs out and then replacing them inside of the vent. It is a very risky process that can lead to multiple health problems such as: internal bleeding, bruising of the sex organs, prolapsing of the vent, damaging of the vent or intestines and an increased chance of infection. Due to the dangerous nature of probing we feel it is necessary to reiterate the fact that this process should NOT be performed by anyone other than a trained PROFESSIONAL – learning the sex of your bearded dragon is not worth risking the plethora health complications probing raises.

Diet

In the wild bearded dragons are omnivores and will eat anything they find. An example of a common diet for a wild bearded dragon would be insects (such as crickets, spiders and worms) and any form of readily available plant matter.

Availability

Bearded dragons are common household pets and are therefore available from pet stores, reptile expos and from specialized breeders. It is best practice to purchase a captive-bred lizard as they are generally healthier and more accustomed to captivity and handling. There are a wide of color morphs available to purchase (although it has to be noted that nonstandard color morphs are more expensive than 'normal' colored lizards).

BEARDED DRAGONS AS PETS

Bearded dragons are one of the most popular lizard species to be kept as household pets. As previously mentioned bearded dragons have an interesting physical appearance and a hardy nature which definitely aids in their popularity. Bearded dragons also have a very docile nature which is a further reason that they make fantastic household pets.

Before Purchase

Before purchasing your bearded dragon it is best practice to set up and heat your vivarium for a minimum of a week before introducing a bearded dragon into it. This will allow for your vivarium to heat to the desired temperature and for you to check that the lighting and humidity are correct for your bearded dragon's needs.

Choosing a Bearded Dragon

While purchasing your bearded dragon it is important to note that juvenile bearded dragons are more likely to become ill or overly stressed during the transportation process. It is therefore best practice to only purchase a bearded dragon that is over 6 inches (15cm) in length to minimize the chance of stress. While choosing your bearded dragon it is important to also choose a bearded dragon that looks alert. As your approach the bearded dragons enclosure the lizard should lift its head and watch you with bright, alert and interested eyes. The last thing to check for during the purchasing process is if the bearded dragon has any visible physical deformities. Physical deformities include burns, sores, pus and external parasites. Some bearded dragons may have toes missing or parts of their tails missing but this is not necessarily anything to worry about as long as the wounds look healed and uninfected.

Transporting your Lizard

It is important to know how to correctly transport your lizard as you will need to transport it after purchase and for any visits to the vet. The safest way to transport your lizard is to place your lizard into an appropriately sized and ventilated plastic container. For added comfort, and to further avoid injury, you can line the container with absorbent and soft paper. It is important to keep the transportation container warm. A good way to keep the temperature of the container warm is to use a heat pack during the transportation process. It is best practice to keep transit time to a minimum to reduce the chance of your lizard becoming stressed.

Handling

It is important to handle your bearded dragon at least once a day. As a species they are naturally curious and appear to enjoy human company. Regular handling is an enjoyable activity for both the lizard and owner and also helps to minimize stress during enclosure cleaning and trips to the vet. Bearded dragons are hardy and can therefore be picked up simply by placing your hand underneath the lizard's belly and gently lifting it up. While handling let the dragon lay on your palm and to keep it secure it is best practice to lightly curly your fingers around the lizard's abdomen. To avoid dropping your lizard it is also advisable to place your free hand below your lizard to catch it in case it falls. Bearded dragons have rough skin which can cause light scratches. To avoid any unwanted scratches it is advisable to wear long sleeves during the handling process.

Toenail Trimming

It is important to trim your bearded dragon's toenails every few weeks as they will natural become needle sharp – which is problematic during the handling process! To trim your lizard's toenails it is best practice to wrap your lizard in a towel while leaving one leg exposed at a time. You can use human nail clippers during the trimming process. It is IMPORTANT to note that bearded dragons have a vein that run through their fingers called a 'quick.' If you cut off too much of your lizard's nail it is possible to cut into the 'quick' which will cause your lizard to bleed. Although not fatal it is still to be avoided as it will cause your pet unnecessary discomfort. If you do accidentally cut the 'quick' you should stop the bleeding by dabbing a little cornstarch onto the nail with a cotton swab. It is also possible to file your lizard's nail or have a vet cut your lizard's nails for you (although this will have a fee). If you are worried about trimming your lizard's nails we recommend taking your lizard to a vet once to have they demonstrate how to trim your pet's nails correctly.

Body Language

During breeding season, or if your bearded dragon feels threatened, it may puff out it's beard. The process of puffing out it's beard is to make the lizard appear larger than it actually is. This act may be accompanied by the lizard 'gaping' it's mouth to again make itself seem larger than it actually is – 'gaping' normally only occurs during fights over territory. Bearded dragons are also known to 'wave' one of their front legs as a sign of submission.

Hygiene

It is best practice to provide your bearded dragon with a bath once a week. The bathing process will help to keep your bearded dragon hydrated as well as helping with the shedding process. Bather water should be warm on your wrist but not hot – the water temperature should be similar to a bath that you would run for a small child. It is important to only make the water as deep as your dragon's chest and to never leave your lizard unattended in the water – drowning and other accidents only take an instance to occur. It is a good idea to disinfect the tub used for bathing after the process is completed as it is not uncommon for the lizard to defecate during the bathing process.

Recording

It is highly advisable to keep a record throughout your bearded dragon's life. By regularly noting down weight, length and feeding patterns you will have a useful resource to help notice any potential problems with your bearded dragon and to likewise make sure it is in good health.

CAN MULTIPLE BEARDIES BE HOUSED TOGETHER?

It is not considered best practice to house multiple bearded dragons in the same vivarium as there is the potential for multiple problems. However some owners have housed multiple bearded dragons together without any issues. This section will outline the best practices for housing multiple beardies together to help you make the best choice for your individual case.

Potential Dangers

There are numerous dangers of housing multiple bearded dragons together. If the bearded dragons are not of a similar size there is the potential for the larger lizard to dominate the food sources which can lead to the smaller lizard, or lizards, becoming underweight and stressed. Close quarters also means the spread of disease or illness is far more likely – which would potentially mean that you would have to spend twice as much at the vets! If housing lizards of differing sexes there is also the potential for unexpected breeding to occur. During the breeding process it is not uncommon for the male to become overly aggressive which can cause both physical harm and stress in the female.

Best Practice when Housing Multiple Beardies

If you choose to house multiple bearded dragons together it is important to have a large vivarium to allow the lizards to have more space to themselves. Housing your lizards in a large vivarium also has the benefit of lowering the chance of aggression due to the fact that the lizards do not have to be in direct contact with each other at all times. It is also important to house lizards of a similar size together for the reasons previously mentioned. Males tend to be more aggressive and territorial so it is best to not house multiple male bearded dragons in the same vivarium. If you are choosing to house multiple dragons together it is best practice to monitor them closely to make sure that there are no issues.

HOUSING

When looking to purchase a vivarium for your bearded dragon it is important to remember that any vivarium designed for juvenile beardies will be outgrown quickly so it is advisable to purchase an adult-sized vivarium from the outset. This section will address the best practices for housing your bearded dragon.

Vivarium Specification

A hatching can be housed in a 20-gallon aquarium for a short time – but as previously mentioned they will quickly out grown this. A 35-gallon aquarium is considered best practice for a single bearded dragon. As previously mentioned when housing more than one bearded dragon together the bigger the enclosure the better – but as a rule a 75-gallon aquarium or vivarium is a decent size to house two beardies together. Bearded dragons cannot climb the glass walls of their enclosures so a lid to the vivarium is not necessary. However it is strongly recommended that you still purchase a vivarium with a lid if you will be housing your bearded dragon in an environment which contains other house hold pets or small children. A lid to the vivarium also prevents insects from being able to escape which is a bonus. It is important that the vivarium you choose to house your bearded dragon in is easy to clean to avoid the buildup of bacteria.

'Furniture'

Bearded dragons enjoy climbing, basking and hiding so it is best practice to create an environment which facilities these needs. Large branches can be provided for climbing. It is important that any branch used within your vivarium is as large, or larger, than your bearded dragon to allow the lizard to bask on it properly. Large flat stones can also be provided for basking purposes. A cardboard box can be used as an inexpensive hide but it is also possible to purchase a specially made hide from a pet store. Plants can be added to the vivarium to provide shade and humidity. Bearded dragons are inquisitive creatures and it is therefore a good idea to change up the layout of your vivarium every few months to allow your bearded dragon to have a 'new' environment to explore.

Cleaning

It is important to keep your vivarium clean as a poorly maintained enclosure can create health risks for your pet. Lizard feces should be cleaned as soon as you spot it as it poses the highest risk of disease or parasites. It is best practice to clean your lizard's vivarium at least once a month with a reptile-safe disinfectant and then to rinse the vivarium well. It is also important to clean your hands before and after cleaning the vivarium and handling your lizard to minimize the chance of infection between both yourself and your lizard.

SUBSTRATES

The term Substrate is defined as being the surface or material on which an organism lives, grows or obtains its nourishment. In terms of bearded dragon care the substrate is what you choose to line your bearded dragon's vivarium. There are multiple different substrates available to use in your vivarium.

Newspaper and Paper Towels

Both newspaper and paper towels are easily obtained and inexpensive. They make for good flooring if your bearded dragon has an injury (for example a severed 'quick') as they are smooth and do not have any potentially harmful edges. However there is the potential for harmful inks to be present within the paper which make them not ideal for long term use.

Artificial Grass

There are many grades of artificial grass which allows you to choose which best suits your lizard's needs. Artificial grass is widely available in hardware stores and ironically the cheapest is normally the best when it comes to lining a vivarium. The cheapest artificial grass tends to be the most flexible which makes it easier to clean as well as cheaper to replace. If artificial grass is used it is best practice to have multiple pieces cut to fit the floor of the vivarium. This allows for you to rotate the flooring when needed to clean and dry the other pieces.

Wood Chippings

Wood chippings are not considered best practice for lining a bearded dragon's vivarium but due to their popularity we have included a section on them. Wood chippings should be avoided for juvenile bearded dragons due to the fact that smaller lizards may have trouble digesting them. If you want to use wood chippings however we recommend using aspen or beech chips. Aspen shavings are decent for lining the floor of your vivarium. A great bonus is that they collect urine and faeces and can easily be scooped out with a dog or cat litter scoop. Aspen shaving only have one flaw and that is that they have to be replaced once they become dirty. However this flaw is inconsequential due to the shavings' relatively low price. Beech chippings are cheap and readily available from all reptile stores. They are not as absorbent as Aspen shavings and likewise need to be removed once they are dirtied. However they come in three different grades – small, medium and large. This allows you to choose which grade best suits your bearded dragon. It is important to note that wood chippings are normally chosen for aesthetic reasons rather than functional reasons.

Oatbran and Wheatbran

Although it sounds like a strange choice to line a vivarium both oatbran and wheatbran are great and inexpensive choices. They a very similar aesthetic as wood chippings but have the benefit of being digestible and dramatically cheaper.

Substrates to Avoid

The following substrates should be avoided due to the fact that they are either toxic or indigestible: cedar shavings, gravel, kitty litter, pesticides and fertilizer.

HEATING AND LIGHTING

All species of reptile require a temperature gradient within their vivarium to allow them to select a temperature that best suits their individual needs at any given moment. It is important to optimize both temperature and lighting to create a comfortable habitat for your bearded dragon.

Primary Heating Source

It is important to place your method of heating on one side of your vivarium to allow for a natural temperature gradient to be created. It is best practice to use an under tank heater (such as the 'Zoo Med Repti Therm U.T.H'). Under tank heaters come in various sizes which allows you to choose the best one to create a temperature gradient within your vivarium. It is likewise important to have a decent thermometer available to check the temperature gradient within your vivarium. It is best practice to use a thermometer which is not fixed to the side of the vivarium. By attaching the thermometer to a wall of the vivarium you will only be measuring the temperature of the air within the tank rather and the temperature of the actual surfaces your lizard resides on. Hot rocks and heat stones are an alternative method of heating your dragon's vivarium.

Hot rocks and heat stones are not considered best practice for heating a reptile vivarium due to the fact that they can potentially become too hot which can lead to the reptile burning themselves. The optimal temperature gradient for a vivarium containing a bearded dragon is 78 degrees Fahrenheit at the cooler end and 88 degrees Fahrenheit at the warmer end (or between 25 and 31 degrees Celsius).

Secondary Heating Source

A secondary heating source, in the form of a 20-75 watt incandescent bulb in a ceramic case, is a great way to create an area in the vivarium for your lizard to bask. When a bulb is being used as a secondary heat source it is best to place a large flat stone underneath it to allow the lizard to bask comfortably. It is likewise important to place the bulb out of reach of your lizard as they may burn themselves against the hot bulbs surface.

Lighting

Reptiles are reliant on natural daylight to set their day and night patterns. Natural sunlight contains UV (ultraviolet) light in two forms, UVa and UVb, that are essential to a bearded dragon's wellbeing. Firstly bearded dragons use UVa to be able to see color. Secondly they use UVb to produce essential vitamin D3 in their skin. D3 is used to store calcium which is an essential mineral for the lizard's health as it prevent metabolic bone disease. UVb does not pass through glass windows and therefore a specialized reptile UVb lamp must be used inside the vivarium itself. You can use either fluorescent or mercury vapor bulbs for your reptile lamp. Fluorescent bulbs need to be replaced every six months as their UVb output diminishes over time. It is important to check that the bulb you choose for your lamp has at least 5 percent UVb (you can locate this information on the lightbulb's packaging. It is important to create a 'photo gradient,' from light to shade, within your vivarium that matches the temperature gradient. Bearded dragons need between 12 and 14 hours of light each day and it is therefore important to remember to turn the reptile light off each night to simulate night.

Brumation

Brumation is a natural energy saving process and is common within adult bearded dragons during the cooler months. It serves a very similar process to hibernation. Brumation is triggered by a reduction in temperature. Bearded dragons will normally eat less and sleep more during this process and it is best practice to closely monitor your lizard during this time.

FEEDING AND WATERING YOUR PET

Bearded dragons are relatively easy to provide for in terms of food and water which makes them an excellent pet for beginner lizard owners. The feeding process is made easier by the fact that their primary food sources are easily obtainable. However the following section will discuss, and explain, some important tips to help optimize the feeding process to keep your lizard as healthy as possible.

What do Bearded Dragons Eat?

As previously mentioned bearded dragons are omnivores which means that they eat both live prey, such as insects, and plant based matter. It is important to give your lizard a balanced diet consisting of both of their food groups. It is best practice to feed juvenile lizards on a diet consisting of mainly insects to help them grow. A juvenile dragon can be fed on a diet that is between 65-80% insects and the other 35-20% being plant matter. It is also not uncommon for owners to feed their bearded dragon's pinkies (baby mice).

How much do Bearded Dragons Eat?

An adult bearded dragon should be fed on between 30 and 50 crickets (or similar sized insects) a week. Best practice for feeding your pet would be in threes: one day salad, one day insects, one day nothing. A juvenile bearded dragon should be fed between 30 and 80 crickets a day. Before the age of 2 to 3 months juvenile bearded dragons should be fed between 3 and 5 times a day. Between the age of 3 and 8 months your lizard should be fed twice a day. After eight months your bearded dragon should be fed once a day. It is important to remove any uneaten insects or plant material.

Pros and Cons of Crickets

The main pros of using crickets as the your pets main food source is the fact that they are nutritionally superior to mealworms and are likewise more active prey which creates a more stimulating feeding process for your bearded dragon. However there are multiple downsides to using crickets as your primary prey choice. Buying crickets in bulk means that you will have to worry about looking after the crickets before using them as prey (which means providing them with food and water). Likewise it is important to note that any large amounts of crickets will produce a significant amount of noise due to their consistent chirping. Another potential negative of using crickets as your primary food choice is the fact that they can easily escape either from the bearded dragon's vivarium or the cage you are keeping the crickets in before they are used as prey. Lastly it is also possible for uneaten crickets to eat your dragon's fecal matter, which will contain harmful parasites, which will then be transferred to your bearded dragon during the feeding process.

Pros and Cons of Mealworms

The main pro of using mealworms as your pet's main source of prey is the fact that they are not very active, they are unable to jump or climb, which means that there is virtually no chance of them escaping. A further benefit of using mealworms is the fact that they can be refrigerated for weeks on end which means that you do not need to worry about feeding and looking after your lizard's prey. It is common practice to server mealworms to your bearded dragon in a small tray which simultaneously eliminates any chance of the worms ingesting the dragon's fecal matter. The tray likewise makes it possible to provide your bearded dragon with a tray of worms on a weekly basis simplifying the feeding process. However there are some negatives of using mealworms. Firstly, as previously mentioned, they are of less nutritional value than crickets and a far less stimulating prey for your lizard. It is possible to increase mealworms activity by introducing a small piece of vegetable to the tray that you place the meal worms in. The introduction of a vegetable allows the mealworms to move around and feed which will help to create a stimulating feeding process for your lizard. Similarly the exoskeleton of mealworms is potentially harder to digest than the exoskeleton of crickets.

Gut Loading

The process of 'gut loading' involves feeding your prey of choice before feeding them to your bearded dragon. The purpose of gut loading is to increase the nutritional value of the prey by feeding them food high in nutrients to transfer the nutrient to your bearded dragon once the prey has been eaten. It is common to feed both crickets and mealworms carrots, oranges, pears and other vegetables for the purpose of gut loading. If you are using mealworms as your prey of choice it is best practice to place your gut loading food in the tray with the worms when you introduce them into the vivarium. This will allow for the mealworms to always be gut loaded and there is a possibility that your bearded dragon will ingest the gut loading food directly while it ingests the mealworms.

Dusting the Prey

It is possible to dust your prey of choice in powders that contain important vitamins and nutrients. To dust your prey of choice effectively place the prey and the powder in either a small can or small bag and shake gently to coat the prey's body in the powder. It is important to shake gently as you do not wish to kill the prey as this may make the bearded dragon disinterested in eating it. It is likewise important to make sure that the prey does not have copious amounts of dust on its body to avoid the chance of dust getting into your lizard's eyes which could lead to an infection.

Pinkies and Waxworms

Both pinkies and waxworms are high in calories and are therefore a great way to increase your bearded dragon's weight if they are underweight. It is common for bearded dragons to lose weight during periods of sickness and it is not uncommon for female dragons to lose weight during the breeding process – primarily after they have laid their eggs. Both pinkies and waxworms should not be the main source of feeding for your lizard as it is possible for bearded dragons to become obese which leads to multiple health problems.

Plant Based Food

A fully grown bearded dragon should be fed on a diet of primarily plant based matter and calcium rich leafy greens and vegetables should make up the bulk of this. The best greens and vegetables to include in a salad for your bearded dragon are: watercress, rocket, cress, dandelion, clover, red and green bell peppers, green beans, acorn squash, lentils, peas, pumpkin, plantain leaves, grated butternut squash and parsley. It is best to avoid giving your bearded dragon kale, cabbage and spinach as too much will prevent calcium absorption and can create a hormonal imbalance within your lizard. Spraying your vegetables and greens with water before serving them to your lizard helps them stay fresh for longer. It is best practice to shred your vegetables and salad into a mixture to help encourage your bearded dragon to eat a variety of food.

Treats

Bearded dragons will appreciate a 'treat' food every once in a while to add a variety to their diet. The following list of foods are a great choice of a 'treat' but should not be used as a primary food source due to high sugar content: apples, bananas, berries, cantaloupe, grapes, mangos, pears, peaches and other similar fruits.

Not Eating?

You should not be alarmed if your bearded dragon does not eat every day. It is not uncommon for bearded dragons to not eat for up to three days during the shedding process. However if your lizard has not eaten for three days and there is no sign of the shedding process taking place it is best to take your lizard to the vet to make sure that it is not ill.

Watering

It is important to provide your bearded dragon with fresh water on a daily basis as bearded dragons will often defecate in their water bowls. Offer the water in a shallow bowl to avoid the chance of your bearded dragon drowning. After placing the water dish into the vivarium it is best practice to swirl your fingers through the dish a few times to create ripples. As previously mentioned bearded dragons are inquisitive creates and the movement created by the ripples will pique their curiosity and encourage them to drink. If your bearded dragon is uninterested in drink it is best practice to spray them lightly with water – they will lick the droplets of their skin to hydrate themselves.

SHEDDING

Like all reptiles and amphibians, bearded dragons shed their skin. Bearded dragons will not shed their entire skin in a single shedding process but will rather shed their skin in large pieces. Juvenile beardies will shed their skin much more frequently than adult dragons due to the fact that they are still growing and will need to shed their skin as they outgrow it.

How to tell if your Bearded Dragon is about to Shed

If your bearded dragon's coloring has suddenly become duller do not worry. The dulling of skin is a good indicator that your lizard is about to shed its skin and the shedding process should occur within a few days of the dulling process. Do not pull off old skin if it seems stuck as it may damage or pull off new skin forming underneath. If your dragon has a lot of unshed skin it is best practice to bathe your dragon to help loosen the old skin.

A Moist Shelter

A moist shelter can be provided during the shedding process as it provides a higher level of humidity which assists the bearded dragon in the shedding process. A good example of a moist shelter is a Tupperware container lined with cypress mulch or peat moss to create the moisture. If you are planning on introducing a moist shelter during the shedding process it is imperative to make sure that the humidity level of your vivarium does not change dramatically.

BREEDING

Bearded dragons are relatively complicated to breed in comparison to many other household lizard species. The process will involve you owning a vivarium for each of your bearded dragons as well as a vivarium reserved for the mating process, an incubator and a laying box.

Before the Breeding Process

It is important to know the sex of your bearded dragons before you start attempting to make them breed with each other. As previously mentioned sexing bearded dragons is a complicated process and it is recommended to have your lizards sexed by a professional vet before attempting breeding. It is also important to feed your female bearded dragon an increased about of gut loaded and nutrient rich food before initiating the breeding process. It is also best practice to feed your female lizard a supplement rich in vitamin D daily to help ensure that her eggs will be adequately calcified. You will need to prepare your male and female bearded dragon for brumation about two months before the breeding process to optimize their fertility.

Preparing the Breeding Habitat

Although your male and female bearded dragons should only be housed together temporarily it is important that the enclosure is set up for optimal breeding. Firstly the enclosure needs to be large enough to house two adult bearded dragons. Secondly the vivarium has to be set up in a manner similar to each individual bearded dragons regular housing to avoid stressing the lizards. It is best practice to provide a larger than normal flat basking stone to allow your lizards to breed.

Preparing the Lay Box

The lay box sis where your female dragon will lay her eggs. The lay box should be between an 8 gallon and a 10 gallon plastic container with a secure lid that allows for a free flowing air circulation. It is important to fill the box with freshly purchased potting soil that does not contain pesticides. The soil should be damp enough to lightly clump together when dug in to allow for the female to bury her eggs with ease.

The Breeding Process

Place your bearded dragons into the designated breeding enclosure. It will take a minimum of a few hours for your bearded dragons to start mating as they will need some time to adjust to their new surroundings and one another. When the male is ready to breed his beard will darken to black. Both the male and female lizard will begin bobbing their heads to indicate their receptiveness to breed. It is not uncommon for the male to chase the female around the enclosure. Do not be alarmed if the male bites the females neck during the breeding process – the male does this to make sure the female cannot leave before the breeding process is completed. Once the breeding process is completed you should wait around a week before placing each bearded dragon back into their respective vivarium. You should then keep them apart for one week and then place them back together again for another breeding session and to ensure that the breeding has been successful.

The Laying Process

If the breeding process has been successful and your female bearded dragon has become pregnant she may start to pace around her enclosure and dig erratically. It is also not uncommon for pregnant beardies to eat less during their pregnancy. You should be able to visibly see the eggs within the females belly about four to six weeks after the mating process. When your bearded dragon exhibits this behavior it is best practice to gently move her to the designated lay box so she can lay her eggs. Once in the lay box your bearded dragon will begin digging to create an area to lay her eggs. You may not be able to tell straight away if she has laid her eggs if you do not actually see her lay them. Once a female has laid her eggs her belly will deflate and become flat again. Once the eggs have been laid it is best practice to quickly move your bearded dragon back into their vivarium. It is most common for eggs to be laid between late afternoon and early evening so this is the best time to watch out for the laying process. Most females will lay around 24 eggs at a time – but can also lay as few as 15 and as many as 50. If your bearded dragon has been in the lay box for multiple days without laying eggs she might be suffering with egg binding – if this is the case you should take your bearded dragon to the vet IMMEDIATELY.

Incubation

Before the laying process it is best practice to prepare your incubator. Make a small thumb impression in the perlite (which should come as standard you're your incubator) which lines the incubator. After they have been laid it is best practice to place the eggs in the incubator as quickly as possible. Lift the eggs gently with your hand and place them in the incubator in a similar orientation to how they were laid. It may be helpful to mark the top of the egg with a pen to prevent you accidently turning the egg upside down. Place one egg into one of the previously made thumb impressions – the egg should fit snuggly. Maintain the incubator temperature between 82 and 86 degrees Fahrenheit. It is important to keep the correct temperature or the embryos inside the egg will most likely die. It is best to follow your individual incubators instruction when it comes to humidity levels as each one is going to be different. It is best practice to check on the eggs about twice a week as it is important to check that they eggs do not have condescension or are overly dry – as both can cause harm to the embryo. Healthy and fertile eggs will increase to about twice their original size and turn a chalky white. Unfertile eggs will turn a pinkish or greenish color.

Hatching

Bearded dragon eggs take between 60 to 70 days to hatch. At around the 60 day mark the eggs may begin to dimple and produce water droplets – do not worry as this is completely normal and indicates that the eggs will be hatching soon. There may also be a slit running the length of the egg which is likewise normal and is created by the baby bearded dragons 'egg tooth' on their snout. It is important to allow the baby bearded dragons to emerge from their eggs on their own which typically takes around 24 to 36 hours. You should keep the newly born bearded dragons in their incubator for the first 24 hours of their life. Sadly during each hatching it is not uncommon for some of the baby dragons to die – if this is the case it is best practice to remove deceased hatchlings are quickly as possible. After they have all hatched you should group the babies together into small tanks (for example 20 gallons) depending on their size. You will not need to feed the hatchlings for the first three days as they are able to survive on the yolk from their eggs. After three days it is important to start providing the babies with a lot of food to help them grow – at this stage it is imperative to remove any dominant bearded dragons to allow the smaller ones to eat as well.

FINAL THOUGHTS

Thank you for purchasing our pet care manual on caring for a bearded dragon. We hope you have found the information both interesting and informative. We hope that this book has allowed you to make an informed choice on whether owning a bearded dragon suits you and if so we hope that the information will help you to provide the best quality care for your pet bearded dragon.

We will be publishing multiple other pet care manuals on our author page on Kindle. If you have an interest in exotic and exciting pets then we highly suggest you check out our other work.

I am passionate about providing the best quality information to our customers. We would highly appreciate any feedback, or reviews, you could leave us on our Kindle page to allow us to help create the best possible pet care products available on the market.

.